5th Grade Workbooks

Geometry & Measurement Practice

AREA

Find the area of the object.
Show your solution on the space provided.

AREA

Find the area of the object.
Show your solution on the space provided.

AREA

Find the area of the object.
Show your solution on the space provided.

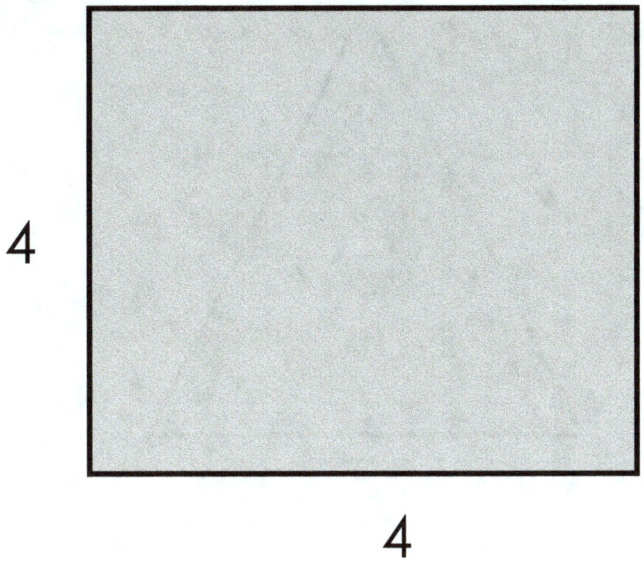

4

4

Find the area of the object.
Show your solution on the space provided.

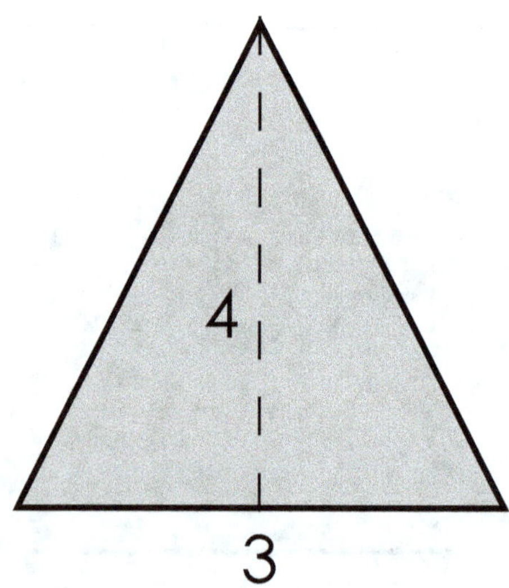

AREA

Find the area of the object.
Show your solution on the space provided.

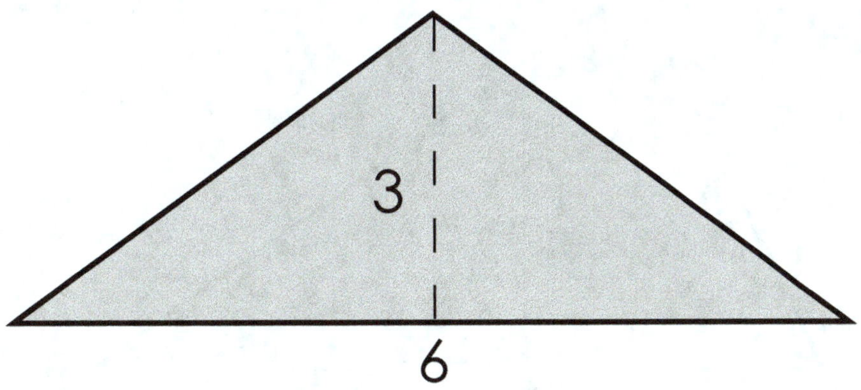

AREA

Find the area of the object.
Show your solution on the space provided.

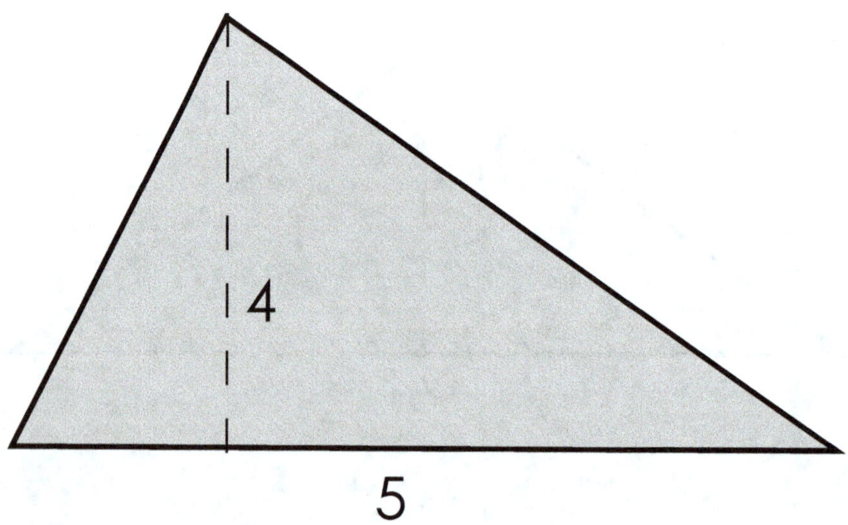

AREA

Find the area of the object.
Show your solution on the space provided.

7

3

AREA

Find the area of the object.
Show your solution on the space provided.

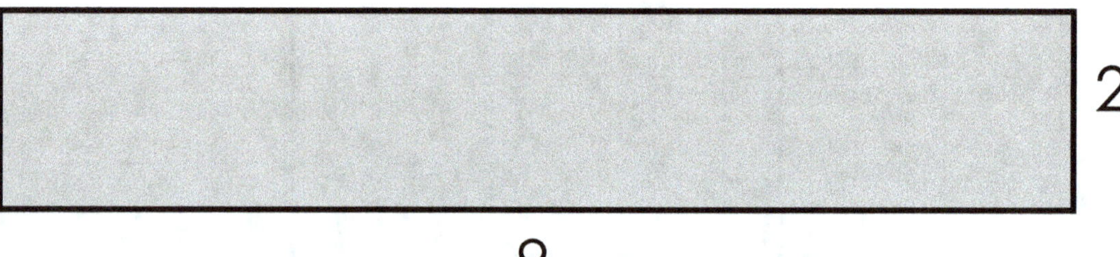

AREA

Find the area of the object.
Show your solution on the space provided.

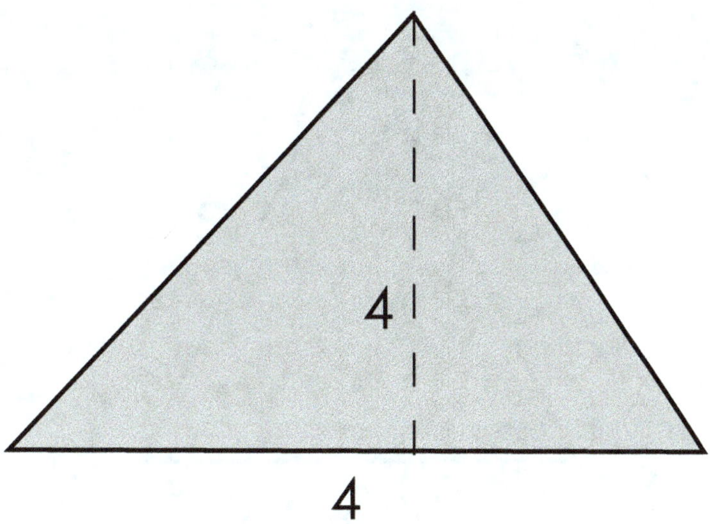

PERIMETER

Find the perimeter of the object.
Show your solution on the space provided.

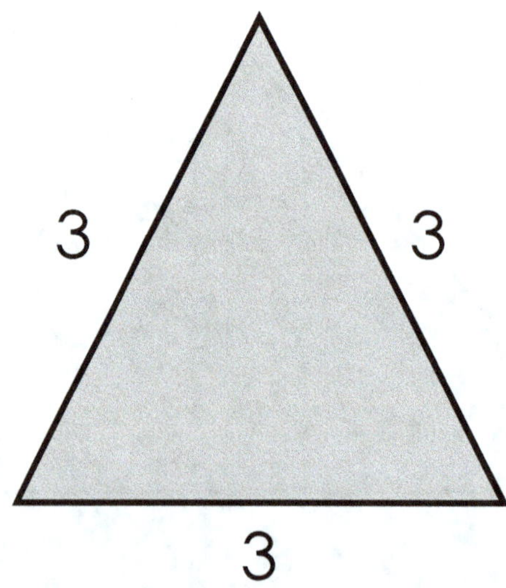

PERIMETER

Find the perimeter of the object.
Show your solution on the space provided.

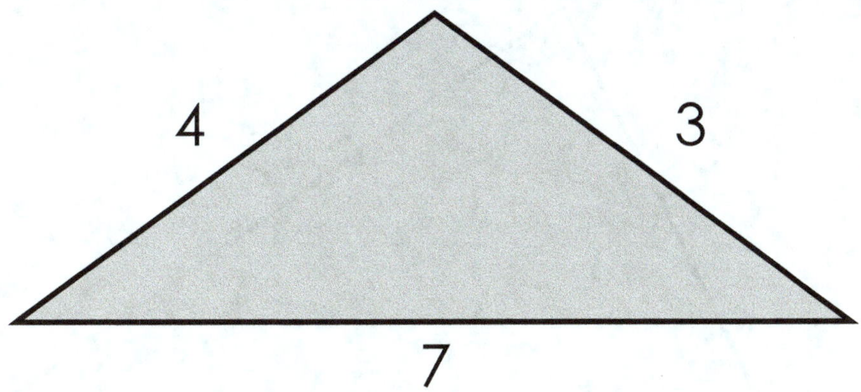

PERIMETER

Find the perimeter of the object.
Show your solution on the space provided.

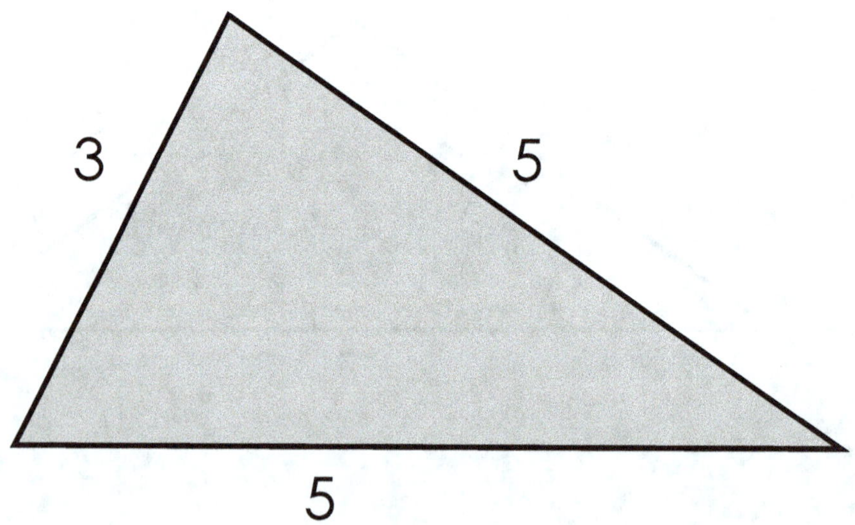

PERIMETER

Find the perimeter of the object.
Show your solution on the space provided.

7

4

PERIMETER

Find the perimeter of the object.
Show your solution on the space provided.

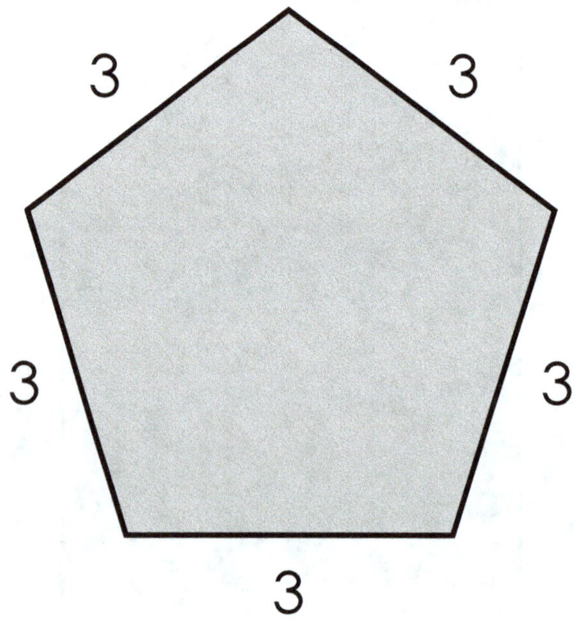

PERIMETER

Find the perimeter of the object.
Show your solution on the space provided.

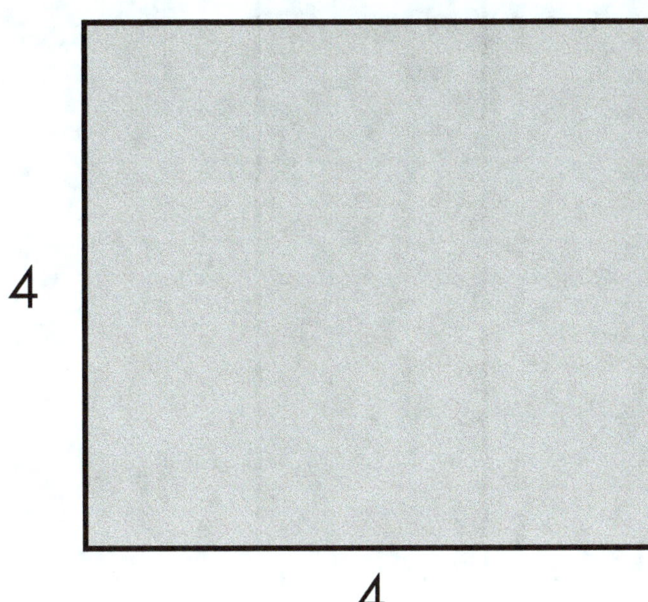

PERIMETER

Find the perimeter of the object.
Show your solution on the space provided.

PERIMETER

Find the perimeter of the object.
Show your solution on the space provided.

PERIMETER

Find the perimeter of the object.
Show your solution on the space provided.

Find the circumference of the circle.
Show your solution on the space provided.

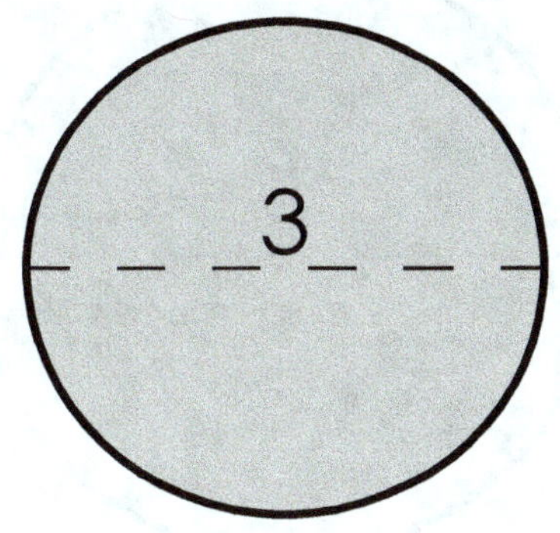

Find the circumference of the circle.
Show your solution on the space provided.

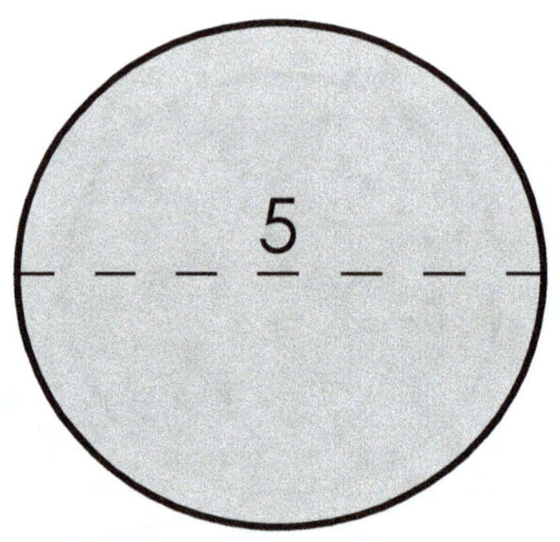

CIRCUMFERENCE

Find the circumference of the circle.
Show your solution on the space provided.

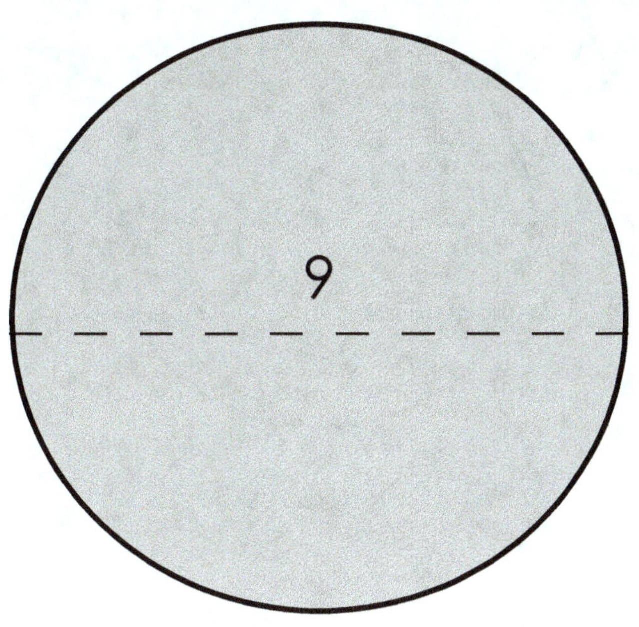

Find the circumference of the circle.
Show your solution on the space provided.

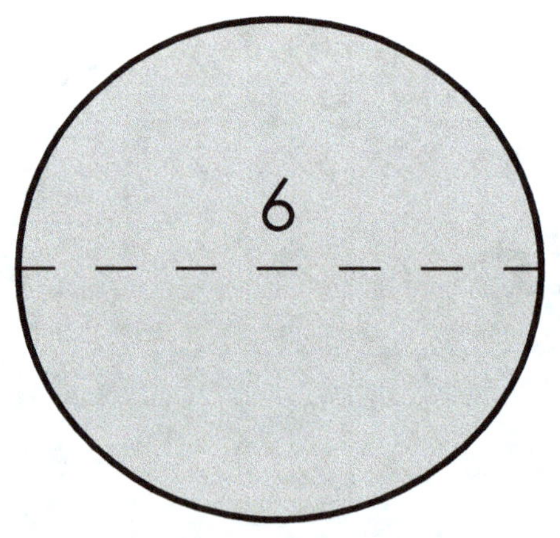

CIRCUMFERENCE

Find the circumference of the circle.
Show your solution on the space provided.

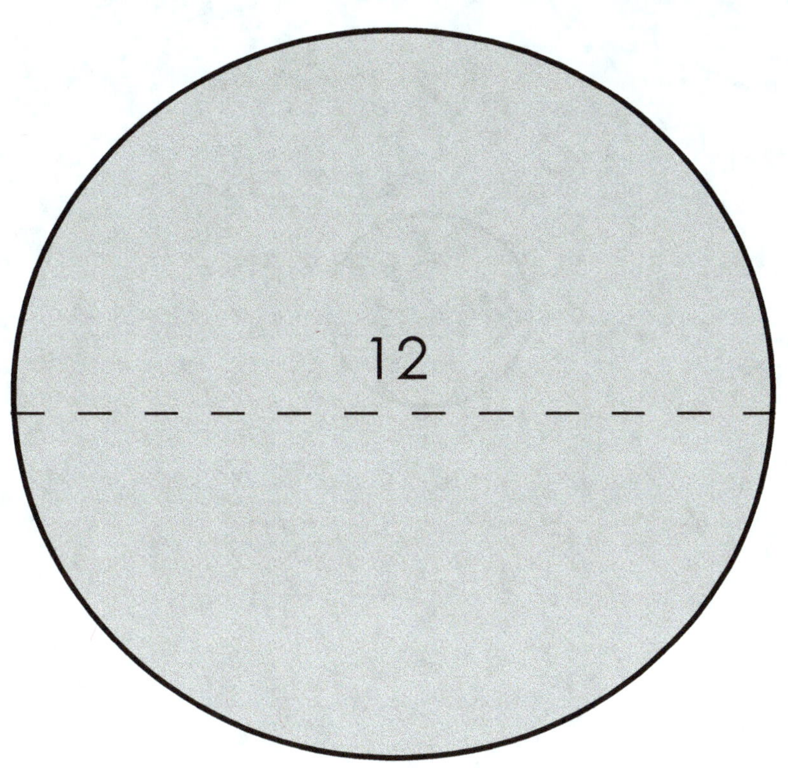

**Find the circumference of the circle.
Show your solution on the space provided.**

CIRCUMFERENCE

Find the circumference of the circle.
Show your solution on the space provided.

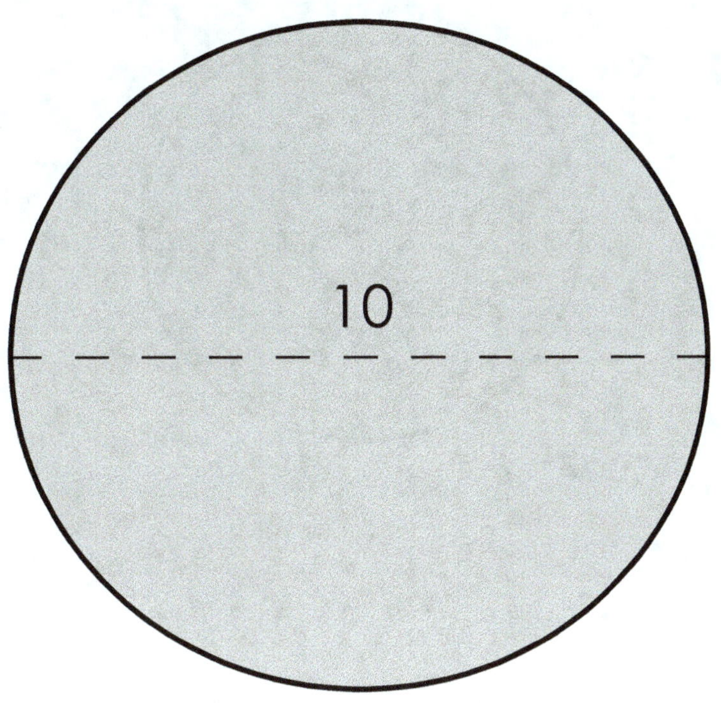

Find the circumference of the circle.
Show your solution on the space provided.

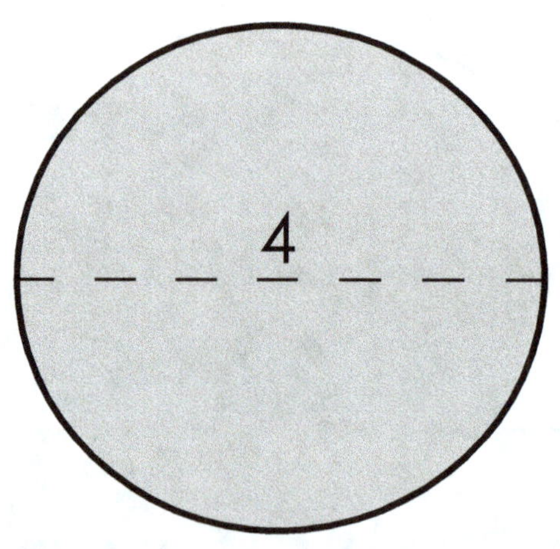

Find the circumference of the circle.
Show your solution on the space provided.

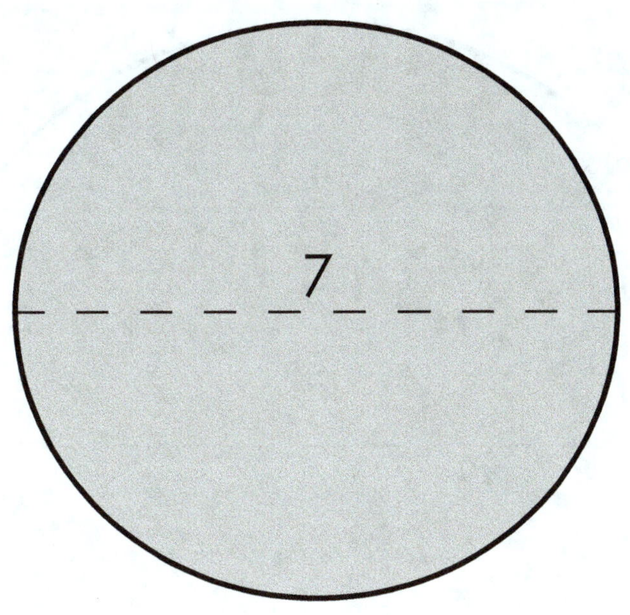

Find the circumference of the circle.
Show your solution on the space provided.

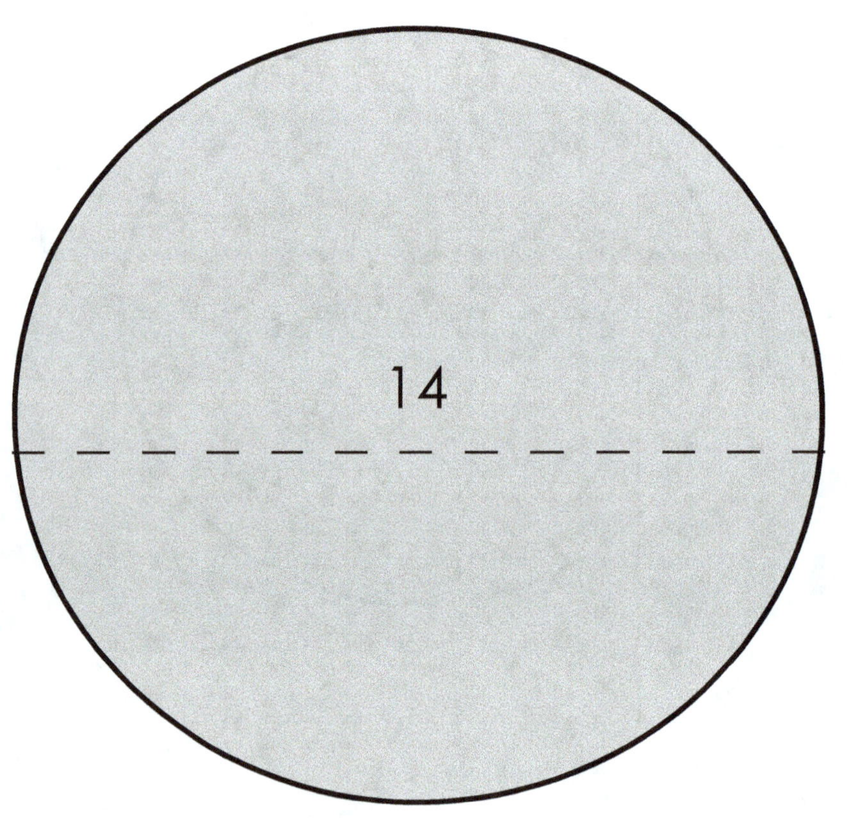

ANSWERS

AREA	PERIMETER	CIRCUMFERENCE
1. **42**	1. **9**	1. **9.42**
2. **24**	2. **14**	2. **15.71**
3. **16**	3. **13**	3. **28.27**
4. **6**	4. **22**	4. **18.85**
5. **9**	5. **15**	5. **37.7**
6. **10**	6. **16**	6. **3.14**
7. **21**	7. **18**	7. **31.42**
8. **18**	8. **12**	8. **12.57**
9. **8**	9. **16**	9. **21.99**
		10. **43.98**